C0-BJI-462

—— *Delicious* ——
T H A I
Cookery

Harveen Choudhary

Nita Mehta
PUBLICATIONS

Delicious
T H A I
Cookery

© Copyright 1999-2006 *Nita Mehta*
PUBLICATIONS

WORLD RIGHTS RESERVED. The contents—all recipes, photographs and drawings are original and copyrighted. No portion of this book shall be reproduced, stored in a retrieval system or transmitted by any means, electronic, mechanical, photocopying, recording or otherwise, without the written permission of the publishers.

While every precaution is taken in the preparation of this book, the publisher and the author assume no responsibility for errors or omissions. Neither is any liability assumed for damages resulting from the use of information contained herein.

TRADEMARKS ACKNOWLEDGED. Trademarks used, if any, are acknowledged as trademarks of their respective owners. These are used as reference only and no trademark infringement is intended upon. Ajinomoto (monosodium glutamade, MSG) is a trademark of Aji-no-moto company of Japan. Use it sparingly if you must as a flavour enhancer.

4th Print 2006
ISBN 81-7676-018-8

Food Styling and Photography: *Nita Mehta*
PUBLICATIONS

Layout and laser typesetting :

National Information
Technology Academy
3A/3, Asaf Ali Road
N.I.T.A. New Delhi-110002
☎ 23252948

Published by :

Nita Mehta
PUBLICATIONS
3A/3 Asaf Ali Road, New Delhi-110002
Tel: 91-11-23250091, 29214011, 23252948, 29218727
Fax:91-11-29225218, 91-11-23250091
E-Mail : nitamehta@email.com, nitamehta@nitamehta.com
Website : http://www.nitamehta.com, http://www.snabindia.com

Distributed by:
THE VARIETY BOOK DEPOT
A.V.G. Bhavan, M 3 Con Circus,
New Delhi - 110 001
Tel : 23417175, 23412567; Fax : 23415335
E-mail: varietybookdepot@rediffmail.com

Printed at:
BRIJBASI ART PRESS LTD.

Rs. 89/-

Foreword

*I*n Thailand, food is a celebration. For a Thai, cooking is a source of pride and wonder. A Thai will always strive for a balance of flavours, texture and colours in a dish, thus creating a combination of flavours — sweet, hot, sour and salty. Thai cuisine is a confluence of Chinese, Malaya and Indian influence, which the Thais have skillfully adapted as distinctly their own.

All the dishes are generally served together at one time and are not eaten in any particular order. However, a soup is always included in the meal but is served along with all the other food. Great emphasis is laid on the presentation, particularly in serving carved vegetables and fruits. The tables are also decorated with these carvings which are a unique form of art.

Thai cooking is simple, quick and healthy. However, some pre-preparation should be done. Get the ingredients you need and make curry pastes well in advance, a few days before your cooking. With this done you will see that it takes hardly any time to zip up a delicious Thai meal.

Happy Cooking!

Contents

Introduction to Thai Cuisine

Thailand's hot and spicy dishes have a unique character of their own. Thai food is characterized by it's exuberant use of hot chillies, garlic, lemon grass, ginger and coconut, which are added to fresh seafood, meat, poultry and vegetables. Coconut milk being a major ingredient, the curries are generally spicy with a hint of slight sweetness. It is an aromatic cuisine due to the use of various herbs and fish sauce. The cooking process is healthy as most of it is quick and stir-fried.

For serving a Thai meal, however, there is no fixed rule. Soup can be served along with the rest of the food, along with snacks or at the beginning of the meal. Steamed rice is generally served at every meal. When planning a Thai meal, prepare one soup, one or two (curry) dishes, one salad and one snack along with steamed rice or any of the other noodles and rice mentioned in the book. The most popular desserts have been mentioned here, however, delicately carved fresh fruits are always served along with the dessert.

Planning a Thai Meal

Preparations to be made in advance :

• Select your menu.

• Prepare the curry paste required, a few days in advance and store in the fridge. It is always better to make extra quantities of the pastes (2-3 times of the recipe), as they can be conveniently stored in the fridge.

• Buy all ingredients needed a day in advance. For good results, try and use fresh ingredients.

• Coconut milk/cream when prepared from a fresh coconut gives the best results. However ready made coconut milk or cream can also be used.

• Prepare coconut milk/cream a day in advance and store in the fridge. They can be covered with a cling film and kept in the fridge for 2-3 days and used as required.

Ingredients Used in Thai Cookery

- **Chillies :** Dry, whole chillies are used for making pastes. Preferably Kashmiri chillies should be used, as these give colour and are not too hot. However any variety can be used. Fresh green ones are also used. When green chillies are kept for a few days they automatically turn red. However, if red are not available, green can be used.

- **Coriander seeds :** *Dhania saboot*

- **Cumin seeds :** *Jeera*

- **Garlic :** *Lahsan*

- **Galangal :** This is the Thai ginger which is used in Thai cooking. Thai use a variety of gingers but these are not available here. If it is not available, using a fresh, tender ginger is good enough. However, the ordinary ginger can also be used without any problem.

- **Lemon grass :** Commonly known as 'Hari chai ki patti' is available with vegetable vendors. Remove the outer fibrous layer. The upper dark green grass like leaves are chewy and can be only used to prepare stocks and soups to which they impart a fragrant lemony flavour. These are discarded before serving. It is only the lower portion of lemon grass which is cut into tiny pieces and used for making curry pastes. You can cut into pieces and store in the fridge for 15-20 days and use whenever needed.

- **Lemon leaves :** These are available with the vegetable vendors. Kaffir lime leaves are the ones that Thai use most. Kaffir is a variety of lime. However, young leaves of any lemon plant can be used.

  Whenever you visit a farm, pluck some lemon leaves and tie in a muslin cloth & keep in the fridge. They will dry up after a few days but impart a delicious flavour whenever used. Can be stored for a few months.

- **Red chilli paste :** Can be made by soaking dried red chillies in hot water for 15-20 minutes and then grinding them to a fine paste.

- **Rice noodles :** These are thin instant rice noodles. As these are precooked, you just have to soak them in warm water for 10-12 minutes. Drain and use.

- **Bean sprouts :** Can be made at home by soaking moong beans (saboot moong dal) for 6-8 hours and then drain and tie in a wet muslin cloth. Keep in a warm place for 1-2 days (depends on the weather) or till well sprouted. Wash and use. However ready sprouts are also available in the market.

- **Mushrooms :** Fresh mushrooms, dried Chinese mushrooms, oyster mushrooms — any of these can be used. However I have used fresh mushroom as these are readily available and taste good.

- **Fish sauce :** Both Indian and Imported sauces are available. Any one of them can be used. It is slightly salty and imparts a lovely flavour to the food. Use less salt in the dish. It does not make the food fishy smelling as the name implies. Do not be scared to use it.

- **Sugar :** Palm sugar is used. However, using ordinary sugar or jaggery (gur) gives equally good results. I have used either sugar or gur in my recipes.

- **Garlic chives :** This is fresh garlic with long green stems.
- **Garlic :** Finely chopped or sliced is the usual way of using it in Thai cooking.
- **Peanuts :** Roasted peanuts without the red skin are used.
- **Basil :** These are sweet basil leaves. Fresh leaves are available in small pouches with vegetable vendors. Dried form is also available. If you are using dried leaves, use a little less as the dried powder is stronger in flavour than the fresh ones. However tender leaves of *'tulsi'* plant can also be used.
- **Coriander :** The Thai use the whole plant including the roots. Wash roots well and use the whole plant. However, only the stem and leaves can be used if roots are not available.
- **Shallots :** Small button onions.
- **Coconut cream :** Can be made from fresh coconut. It is also available in the market in tetra packs.

  From fresh coconut : Grate one coconut. Soak in **1 cup** hot water for 20-

30 minutes. Churn well in the mixer and strain through a muslin cloth to get thick coconut cream, which when kept in the fridge for a few hours, starts to look and feel like fresh cream. The unstrained coconut in the cloth can also be used for making coconut milk by adding another cup of hot water to it.

From powder : Mix ½ **cup** warm water to ½ **cup** powder.

◆ **Coconut milk :** Can be made from fresh coconut. It is also available in the market in tetra packs. It is a chief ingredient of Thai cooking, specially in curries and desserts.

From fresh coconut : Grate one coconut and soak in **3 cups** of warm water for 25-30 minutes. Churn well in the mixer and strain to get coconut milk. The left over coconut after making coconut cream can also be used for making coconut milk.

From powder : Mix ½ **cup** powder with **1 cup** warm water to get coconut milk.

◆ **Tamarind Juice :** Soak 1 rounded tbsp tamarind in 1 cup warm water for 15 minutes. Mash well and strain to get tamarind juice.

¥ ¥ ¥ ¥

Essential Pastes & Sauces

Generally one paste is used in one Thai dish.

¥ ¥ ¥ ¥

Red Curry Paste

Gives 1½ cups

8-10 Kashmiri red chillies - soaked in ½ cup warm water for 10 minutes
1 onion - chopped, 15-20 flakes garlic - peeled, 1½" piece ginger - sliced
2 sticks lemon grass - the lower stem is cut into small pieces, (read p. 12)
3 tbsp chopped fresh coriander
½ tsp peppercorns (saboot kali mirch), 1 tsp salt
1 tbsp coriander seeds (saboot dhania), 2 tsp cumin seeds (jeera)
1 tsp shrimp paste or 1 tbsp vinegar

1. On a tawa, dry roast cumin and coriander seeds on low heat till they become aromatic and get roasted but not brown.
2. Put all the other ingredients and the roasted seeds in a grinder and churn well to get a fine paste.
3. Store in a steel box or a glass jar in the fridge. Can be kept for a few days, about 8-10 days.

Thai Fish Curry : Recipe on page 79 ➤

Green Curry Paste

Gives about ½ cup if using small hot ones (preferably use these)

10-12 hot green chillies
½ onion - chopped
1 tbsp chopped garlic, ½" piece ginger - chopped
2 sticks lemon grass - cut into pieces, 2-3 lemon leaves
½ tsp lemon rind, 4 tbsp coriander leaves
½ tsp salt, 1 tbsp lemon juice, 15 peppercorns (saboot kali mirch)
1 tbsp coriander seeds (saboot dhania), 1 tsp cumin seeds (jeera)

1. In a wok/tawa over low heat, put coriander and cumin seeds. Roast dry for 2 minutes till fragrant but not brown.
2. Put all the other ingredients and the roasted seeds in a blender and blend to a fine paste, using a little water.
3. Can be stored in the fridge in a steel/glass box for a few day (8-10 days).

Roasted Chilli Paste

Gives about ½ cup

20 small, dried red chillies
2 tbsp oil
3 tbsp chopped garlic
1½ cups chopped onion/spring onions or shallots
3 tbsp fish sauce
2 tbsp tamarind juice
2 tsp sugar

1. Heat oil. Add onion, garlic and chillies. Fry till onions turn golden brown.
2. In a blender, add the fish sauce, tamarind juice, sugar, the fried onions, garlic, and chillies.
3. Blend to a fine paste (sauce) using little water if needed.
4. This can be stored in the fridge for a few days (8-10 days).

Masaman Curry Paste

Also called Muslim curry paste

15 dried, red chillies - soak in water for 15-20 minutes
4 tbsp chopped white part of spring onions/onions or shallots
5-6 large flakes garlic (increase the number if flakes are small)
3 stalks lemon grass - cut into pieces
1 tbsp cumin seeds (jeera)
1 tbsp coriander seeds (saboot dhania)
2 tsp chopped ginger
3 cloves (laung), 6 black peppercorns (saboot kali mirch)

1. Roast all ingredients on a tawa/wok for 5 minutes or till fragrant.
2. Grind to a fine paste. Use little water if needed.
3. Can be stored in the fridge for a few days (8-10 days).

Chilli Sauce

Also called Nam Jeem

8 fresh red chillies - chopped
8 garlic flakes - crushed
1 tbsp fish sauce
2 tsp sugar
juice of 1 lime or lemon
¼ tsp salt
½ cup water
2 tbsp groudnut oil

1. Put the chillies, garlic, fish sauce, sugar, lime or lemon juice and the salt in a small saucepan.
2. Stir in the water and oil. Bring to the boil, reudce the heat and simmer gently for 10-15 minutes.
3. Blend until smooth in a food processor or blender. Store in an airtight jar in the refrigerator for a maximum of 2 weeks. Use as required.

¥ ¥ ¥ ¥

Soups

Method for making Chicken Stock/Broth

Bones remaining after making chicken boneless can be used. Use 3-4 pieces of chicken. Add 5 cups water, 2 sticks of celery, a small piece of ginger and 1-2 stalks of lemon grass. Put in a cooker. Give 3-4 whistles. Lower the heat and simmer for 8-10 minutes. Remove from fire. When the pressure drops, strain and use as broth/stock. The chicken can be added to rice or noodles.

¥ ¥ ¥ ¥

Sour & Spicy Chicken Soup

Serves 4

(Tom Yam Kai)

200 gms boneless chicken - cut into very small pieces (diced)
2 tbsp butter, 3 cups chicken stock (page 24)
100 gms mushrooms - sliced
5-6 cherry tomatoes or 1 large tomato - cut into bite size pieces
1 tbsp finely chopped lemon grass stem
1½ tbsp fish sauce, ½ tsp sugar, 2 tbsp lemon juice, salt to taste
5-6 hot chillies - broken with a pestle (use as per taste. First use 2-3 chillies and
if desired, use more)

1. Heat 2 tbsp butter. Add chicken. Fry for 2-3 minutes.
2. Add mushrooms, tomato, lemon grass, chicken stock and all seasonings.
3. Simmer for 6-7 minutes. Adjust seasonings and serve hot garnished with
   slices of deseeded chillies.

Chicken & Coconut Soup

Picture on page 1   *Serves 4*

(Kai Tom Kah)

6 cups chicken stock or water
3 chicken breast portions or 400 gm boneless pieces of chicken
1 onion - finely chopped
2-3 stalks lemon grass - cut into small pieces
3 kaffir lime leaves
1" piece ginger - crushed
2 cups coconut milk
juice of 1 lemon (2 tbsp)
2 tsp brown sugar, 1½ tsp salt, or to taste
2 fresh red chillies - deseeded and chopped
few basil leaves
1-2 tsp soya sauce

1. Bring the chicken stock, breast portions, onions, lemon grass, lemon leaves and ginger to a boil. Cover the pan and simmer for 15-20 minutes.
2. Strain the stock into a clean saucepan. Add the coconut milk, stirring until blended. Bring to the boil and then simmer gently over low heat for 10 minutes.
3. Meanwhile, shred the chicken pieces.
4. Stir the lemon juice, shredded chicken and brown sugar into the soup. Add soya sauce. Simmer for 2-3 minutes, and then serve garnished with red chillies and fresh basil leaves.

Note: Add 2 tsp cornflour dissolved in 2 tbsp water if the soup appears thin. Boil for 2-3 minutes and serve.

Prawn Soup

Picture on facing page　　　　　　*Serves 4-6*

(Meng Tom Yam Kung)

300-350 gm uncooked small prawns
4 cups (1 litre) water
3 small lemon leaves
1 tbsp chopped lemon grass
1 tsp fish sauce
2 tbsp fresh lime juice
2 tbsp chopped coriander leaves
1½ tbsp sliced spring onions
1 red chilli - deseeded and sliced into 1- inch strips
salt and pepper to taste

1. Prepare the prawns, shell them and remove the dark vein running along the back. Wash them under running water, drain and pat dry with absorbent kitchen paper. Set aside while you make the soup.
2. Pour the water into a large saucepan and bring to a boil. Add the lime leaves and chopped lemon grass, reduce the heat and simmer for 10 minutes.
3. Add the fish sauce and cook for a further 5 minutes.
4. Add the prawns and lime juice to the pan and cook gently over very low heat for a few minutes, until the prawns become firm and turn a pale pink colour.
5. Add the chopped coriander leaves, spring onions and red chilli strips to the soup.
6. Check the seasonings, adding salt, pepper and lemon juice, making it really piquant, and serve very hot in small bowls.

Tom Yam Gai Soup

Serves 4

2 chicken breasts - make boneless and cut into small pieces
3 tbsp oil
1 tsp ginger strips, 2 tbsp basil leaves - chopped
8-10 lemon leaves, salt to taste
¼ cup roasted peanuts - ground finely
5 cups chicken broth/stock (page 24)
long slices of red & green chillies for garnishing

PASTE (GRIND TOGETHER)
3 cloves garlic - chopped, 4 peppercorns, 1 tsp coriander leaves

1. Heat oil. Add garlic-pepper paste and chicken. Fry for 3-4 minutes.
2. Add all other ingredients and broth/stock. Simmer for 10-15 minutes.
3. Serve garnished with long slices of red and green chillies.

Note : For a thicker soup, use ½ cup peanuts.

31

¥ ¥ ¥ ¥

Salads

¥ ¥ ¥ ¥

Thai Egg Salad

Serves 4

5 hard boiled eggs
½ cup coarsely chopped green (raw) mango or apple, preferably it should be a
little sour, ¼ cup mint leaves
2 tbsp chopped spring onions or ordinary onion
½ cup shredded cabbage, ½ cup grated carrot
a few lettuce and mint leaves to garnish

DRESSING
3 tbsp lemon juice, 1 green chilli - sliced
2 tbsp chopped garlic, 1 tsp salt, 2 tbsp salad oil or any cooking oil

1. Grind together for the dressing — lemon juice, green chilli, garlic, salt
   and oil. Keep aside.
2. Cut eggs into ½" thick slices or ½" pieces. Mix together all the ingredients.
   Pour dressing on top. Mix well.
3. Serve on a bed of lettuce leaves garnished with mint leaves.

Spicy Sausage Ham Salad

Serves 4-5

This is a very spicy salad. Either frankfurters or cocktail sausages can be used. It can also be served as a snack.

100 gms sausages, 100 gms ham
100 gms roasted cashewnuts
2 tbsp roasted chilli sauce (page 21)
½ tsp salt
¼ cup shredded cabbage
3 tbsp tamarind juice/vinegar
1 tbsp lemon juice
¼ cup sliced onion
2 tbsp butter

GARNISHING
4-5 leaves lettuce
tomato wedges

1. Cut sausages diagonally into slices about 2" thick. Cut ham into ½" pieces.
2. Heat ¼ cup water. Add sausages, boil. When water dries, add 1 tsp oil. Fry for 1-2 minutes but do not brown too much, keep aside.
3. Heat butter. Add roasted chilli paste. Fry for 2-3 minutes or till aromatic and leaves oil. Then add tamarind juice and salt. Boil, remove from heat and add lemon juice.
4. Add ham, sausages, cabbage, onion and cashewnuts. Mix well.
5. Place salad in the centre of a serving platter surrounded with finely chopped lettuce and garnish with tomato wedges.

Southern Thai Salad

Serves 4-5

A delicious salad with a lovely peanut flavour.

3 hard boiled eggs
4-5 lettuce leaves, 1 cup bean sprouts
2 cups chopped (½" pieces) cucumber
1 cup chopped (½" pieces) tomato
2 tbsp lemon juice, salt to taste
oil for frying
1 potato peeled - for garnishing

DRESSING

2 dried red chillies whole - soaked in warm water 15 minutes
¼ cup sliced shallots/onion, ½ cup roasted peanuts
yolks of 3 boiled eggs (from hard boiled eggs given above)
3 tbsp fish sauce, 1 tbsp sugar
¼ cup tamarind juice

2 tbsp butter
1 cup coconut milk, ¼ tsp salt, ¼ tsp haldi
¼ tsp red chilli powder - (increase if you want the salad to be hot)

1. For the dressing, grind together chillies, peanuts, shallots/onion, egg yolks (boiled), fish sauce, sugar, tamarind juice and oil. Grind to a fine paste. Use little coconut milk for grinding if needed.
2. Heat butter. Add salt, red chilli powder and haldi. Add coconut milk.
3. Add the ground paste and cook till thick, (like mayonnaise). Keep the dressing aside.
4. For the salad, peel and cut potato into very thin slices. Soak for 5 minutes in salted water. Drain. Deep fry till crisp golden brown, keep aside.
5. Cut cucumbers, onions, tomatoes and white of hard boiled eggs into ½" pieces.
6. Put bean sprouts in hot water for 5 minutes. Drain.
7. Mix everything with the dressing, except potatoes. Adjust salt to taste.
8. Arrange lettuce leaves on a platter. Spoon salad on it. Garnish with chopped green or red chillies, fried potatoes and serve chilled.

Note : Garnish at the time of serving, otherwise potatoes will get soggy.

Larp of Chiang Mai

Serves 5-6

(Savoury Chicken Salad)

Chiang Mai is a city in the North east of Thailand and is famous for it's chicken salad. However, instead of chicken, mutton or pork mince can also be used.

200 gms (1½ cups) chicken keema
1 onion - chopped
2 tsp oil
1 tsp salt
2 tbsp prepared red curry paste or 1-1 ½ tsp readymade red chilli paste
2 tbsp fish sauce
2 spring onions (10 tbsp) finely chopped
2 tbsp fresh chopped coriander
2-4 tbsp lemon juice, to taste
½ cup mint leaves - chopped
6 tbsp roasted ground rice (see note on the next page) or bread crumbs

GARNISHING
some salad leaves, cucumber & tomato slices and a few sprigs of mint

1. Heat oil. Add onion. Fry for 1-2 minutes.
2. Add keema, chilli paste or curry paste and salt.
3. Fry for 2-3 minutes. Add ½ cup water. Cover and cook on low heat for 5-7 minutes or till cooked. (If using mutton keema, give 2-3 whistles in the pressure cooker). Increase heat and dry the keema.
4. Add all ingredients along with ground rice or bread crumbs.
5. Mix well. Serve on a bed of lettuce or cabbage leaves, garnished with cucumber and tomato slices and sprigs of mint.

Note : *Method for making ground roasted rice:*
Cook rice. Put rice in a frying pan and dry roast until golden brown. Grind to a fine powder. Keep in an air tight jar and use as required.

¥ ¥ ¥ ¥

Snacks

¥ ¥ ¥ ¥

¥ ¥ ¥ ¥ ¥
¥
¥
¥
¥

Fragrant Thai Meat balls

Gives 24-25 balls

These tasty meat balls can be made from minced mutton or pork or chicken.

500 gms mince
1 tbsp chopped garlic
4-5 spring onions - finely chopped or 2 medium onions - chopped
1 tbsp chopped fresh coriander, 4-5 tbsp red curry paste (page 18)
1 tbsp lemon juice, 1 tbsp fish sauce (optional)
1 tsp salt, or to taste, ½ tsp pepper, 1 egg, rice flour for dusting
oil for deep frying, sprigs of coriander for garnishing

1. Wash mince. Squeeze out all the water.
2. Mix all ingredient except rice flour and oil. Churn or grind in the mixer or mix well with hands.
3. Make balls, roll in the rice flour and deep fry all together on low heat till golden and the mince gets cooked. Serve hot, garnished with coriander.

Note : Instead of rice flour, powdered bread crumbs or suji can be used for rolling meatballs.

Ӽ Ӽ Ӽ Ӽ Ӽ Ӽ Ӽ Ӽ Ӽ

Thai Chicken Satay

Picture on page 1　　　　*Serves 6*

(Chicken on Skewers)

400 gm chicken - bite sized boneless pieces
6 bamboo skewers - soaked in water to prevent burning

MARINADE

1 tsp salt, ½-1 tsp red chilli powder
2 tsp brown sugar, 2 tsp oil
3-4 tbsp coconut milk , 1 tbsp lemon juice, 2 tsp soya sauce
8-10 flakes garlic - crushed to a paste
1½ tsp jeera powder (ground cumin), 1½ tsp dhania powder

PEANUT SAUCE

¼ cup (50 gm) roasted salted peanuts, ½ tsp salt
1 tsp oil, 4-6 flakes garlic - crushed
½ tsp red chilli powder, ½-1 tsp sugar, 1½ tsp lemon juice
1 tsp soya sauce, 1 cup coconut milk

1. Mix all the marinade ingredients thoroughly, add chicken pieces to it and mix very well. Leave aside for 1-2 hours in the refrigerator.
2. Thread marinated chicken pieces onto oiled wooden skewers. Leave behind the marinade.
3. Cook in a preheated grill at 230°C for 10-11 minutes, turning them once in between and basting with the remaining marinade. Alternately, heat a non-stick flat tawa, grease it slightly with a few drops of oil and place skewered chicken, a few at a time. Cook on high heat, turning them frequently. Cook till soft.
4. To make peanut sauce, grind peanuts with the salt to a rough powder.
5. Heat oil in a heavy bottomed small pan or kadhai. Add garlic. Saute till it starts to change colour. Reduce heat. Add red chilli powder. Add only ½ cup coconut milk. Boil, stirring. Cook on low heat for 3 minutes, stirring constantly. Stir in the crushed peanuts, sugar, lemon juice, soya sauce and the remaining ½ cup coconut milk. Boil. Simmer gently for 5 minutes, stirring occasionally to prevent it sticking to the pan. Transfer to a bowl.
6. Serve satay accompanied with the peanut sauce.

Golden Pouches

Gives 15 pouches

These crisp delicious pouches are served as an appetizer or as an accompaniment with drinks.

POUCHES
1 cup maida
½ cup suji
a pinch of soda-bicarb
½ tsp salt
1 tbsp oil

FILLING
1 tbsp butter/oil
225 gms mince (mutton or chicken or pork)
1 tbsp chopped fresh coriander
½ to 1 tbsp chopped garlic
2 tbsp chopped spring onion/onion

¥ ¥ ¥ ¥ ¥
¥
¥
¥
¥

½ tsp salt or adjust to taste
1 tbsp fish sauce
1 tsp sugar/gur
1 tsp red chilli paste or chill powder
8-10 long chives (fresh garlic) chopped (optional)
some freshly ground pepper (optional)

1. Mix all ingredients of the pouches and make a dough with water (like chapati dough). Keep aside covered.
2. Heat oil in a cooker. Add garlic. Fry for 1-2 minutes.
3. Add mince, salt, red chilli paste and 3-4 tbsp water.
4. Give 3-4 whistles. Cool and open the cooker. Add all the other ingredients, seasonings and cook til it dries completely.
5. Cool, adjust seasonings to taste and keep aside.
6. Make small balls around 15 and roll one at a time into a small rounds.
7. Put filling in the centre and pick up the sides and press at the neck to form a money pouch. Tie the neck with a thin lemon grass.
8. Deep fry 5-6 pieces at a time on medium flame to a golden brown colour.
9. Serve hot with sauce or any of the dips of your choice.

᚛ ᚛ ᚛ ᚛ ᚛ ᚛

Fish Cakes with Cucumber Relish

Picture on facing page   Makes 12-14 cakes (patties)

A great favourite of my family. These wonderful small fish cakes are a familiar and a very popular appetizer of Thailand.

300 gm fish - cut into small pieces, boneless and preferably skinless
1 star anise, 1" stick cinnamon (dalchini), 2-3 lemon leaves
5-6 tbsp red curry paste (page 18) or 2 tsp red chilli paste
1 egg
50 gms beans (French beans) - chopped finely
6 tbsp cornflour
2 tbsp fish sauce
2-3 big flakes of garlic - chopped
1 tsp salt
½ tsp sugar/gur
3 lemon leaves - shredded or cut into very small pieces (optional)
2 tbsp coriander leaves chopped

CUCUMBER RELISH (GIVES 1¼ CUPS)

4 tbsp vinegar, 4 tbsp water
2 tbsp sugar, 1 tsp salt, 2-3 flakes garlic - paste or minced
1 small cucumber - cut into thin slices or very small pieces
5 tbsp/4 shallots/1 small onion - finely sliced or chopped
½ tbsp finely chopped ginger, 2 green/red chillies - sliced

1. To prepare the relish, cook together vinegar, water, sugar and salt. When sugar dissolves, give 2-3 boils and remove from heat. Cool.
2. Add all the other ingredients and mix well. Keep relish aside.
3. Heat a pan of water with anise, cinnamon and lemon leaves.
4. When it boils, add fish. Let it cook for 4-5 minutes. Remove fish from water, when skin can be removed easily. Remove skin. (If using skinless fish it can be used raw).
5. Put fish, egg and curry paste in the mixer and churn well to get a smooth mixture. Transfer to a bowl. Mix all other ingredients including beans & cornflour. Mix well. Shape into small patties & deep fry till golden brown.
6. Serve hot with cucumber relish or any other sauce or dip of your choice.

Note : If patties break on frying, increase the cornflour by 1-2 tbsp.

Spring Rolls

Gives 18 rolls

Spring rolls are as popular in Thai cuisine as they are in Chinese.

FILLING
1 tbsp oil
½ -1 tbsp chopped garlic
200 gms minced meat (mutton, chicken or pork)
6 large mushrooms
50 gms rice noodles
1 tsp red chilli paste or red chilli powder
1 tsp salt
½ cup bean sprouts
2 tbsp fish sauce (optional)
2-3 green chillies - chopped, 1 tbsp chopped coriander leaves
1 tsp sugar
½ cup/2 spring onions - chopped
½ cup grated carrot

WRAPPERS

2¼ cups maida
3 eggs
¾ tsp salt
1½ cups water
oil for frying

1. Heat oil in a pressure cooker. Add garlic and fry for 1-2 minutes.
2. Add mince, red chilli paste, salt and a little water (3-4 tbsp).
3. Give 3-4 whistles. Cool. Open the pressure cooker.
4. Soak rice noodles in warm water for 10-12 minutes. Drain.
5. Add noodles, all seasonings and other ingredients like chillies, bean sprouts, mushrooms, carrot, spring onions, coriander leaves, sugar etc. to the cooked mince. Heat and dry completely. Cool the filling.
6. For the wrappers, sift maida and salt.
7. Add egg, mix well.
8. Add enough water gradually beating well to get a smooth batter of a pouring consistency. However, if batter gets lumpy, sieve it.

9. Heat a lightly greased non stick tawa/pan. Remove pan from fire and pour 2 tbsp batter on it and tilt the pan to spread the batter. Return to fire.
10. Remove from tawa when the under side is cooked. Do not cook the other side.
11. Cool pancakes on a dry clean cloth with cooked side up.
12. Place a little filling on the cooked side of the pancake.
13. Fold in the right and left sides and roll. Seal edges with cornflour/maida paste made by mixing little cornflour or maida with little water.
14. Heat oil in a pan and fry rolls till golden brown. Drain on absorbent paper. Serve whole or cut diagonally into pieces and serve hot with any of the dips.

¥ ¥ ¥ ¥

Noodles & Rice

¥ ¥ ¥ ¥

Stir Fried Noodles

Serves 2-3   *Picture on cover*

100 gms thin, flat, rice noodles
½ tbsp chopped garlic
100 gms boneless chicken - cut into small strips
1 cup mixed vegetables (4-5 small florets cauliflower or broccoli, 2 baby corns,
½ carrot, ¼ capsicum) - cut into thin long pieces
1 tsp red chilli paste (page 13) or 2-3 tbsp red curry paste (page 18)
2 whole, red chillies (dried or fresh) - chopped
¼ cup bean sprouts, optional
1 spring onion - chopped (the greens are cut into 1" pieces)
1 tbsp fish sauce
½ tsp sugar, ½ tsp salt, 2-3 tbsp tamarind juice or vinegar
2 tbsp roasted peanuts - coarsely ground
4 tbsp oil

1. Soak noodles in warm water for 10-12 minutes. Rinse in cold water. Drain and keep aside.
2. Heat 2 tbsp oil in a wok/pan. Add garlic. Fry till golden brown.
3. Add chicken. Fry for 3-4 minutes. Add broccoli and baby corns. Saute for a minute. Add ½ tsp salt and cover and cook for about 4-5 minutes till chicken and vegetables turn tender. Remove from wok and keep aside.
4. In the wok, again heat 2 tbsp oil. Add chopped red chillies. Fry for 1-2 minutes. Add red chilli paste or curry paste. Fry for about 2-3 minutes till aromatic and leaves oil.
5. Add bean sprouts and spring onions. Fry for 1 minute.
6. Add chicken and vegetables, capsicum and carrots, noodles, fish sauce, salt, sugar, vinegar and peanuts. Mix well. Serve hot.

Masaman Curried Chicken Rice

Serves 4-5   *Picture on page 57*

Delicious aromatic rice which can be had plain without any other dish. Is a complete meal by itself almost like a masala chicken biryani.

1 cup basmati rice (soaked for 10-15 minutes)
½ cup french beans - diced
½ cup carrots - diced
½ capsicum - diced
250 gms chicken - If using boneless cut into strips, if using with bones, cut into small pieces
3 tbsp oil
4-5 tbsp masaman paste (page 22)
½ cup coconut cream
1½ tsp salt, ½ tsp haldi powder
2 stalks lemon grass - tie into a knot, discard when rice is ready
2-3 tbsp lemon juice
1 cup coconut milk

1. Heat oil. Add masaman curry paste. Fry till aromatic and leaves oil.
2. Add chicken. Fry for 2-3 minutes. Add coconut cream. Heat till nearly dry.
3. Add vegetables and all other ingredients, 1 cup water, 1 cup coconut milk and soaked rice.
4. Cover. After one boil, lower heat and cook covered for 8-10 minutes or till all the water has dried and the rice is cooked.
5. Discard lemon grass.
6. Serve hot garnished with fresh coriander, lemon wedges and tomato slices.

Masaman Curried Chicken Rice : Recipe on page 55 ➤

Chiang Mai Noodles

Serves 4-5

A signature dish of the city of Chiang Mai. If kept thin, can be had as a soup also.

100 gms egg noodles - boiled
300 gms chicken - cut into bite size pieces
2 tbsp oil, 2 tbsp butter
4-5 tbsp red curry paste (page 18)
1 tbsp soya sauce, 4 tbsp fish sauce
1 cup stock/water (If serving as soup increase it to 2½ cups)
2 cups coconut milk
¼ tsp each salt, pepper, 1 tsp turmeric/haldi powder
juice of ½ lemon (1 - 1 ½ tbsp)

GARNISHING

2-3 spring onions - chopped along with the green part
4-5 green/red chillies - deseeded & chopped
2-3 tbsp chopped fresh coriander leaves
2 tbsp fried sliced garlic

1. Heat oil and butter. Add haldi and curry paste. Fry for about 2-3 minutes till aromatic and leaves oil.
2. Add chicken. Fry for 3-4 minutes.
3. Add ½ cup coconut milk. Cover and cook till chicken is tender.
4. Add fish sauce, soya sauce, salt, pepper, water/stock and 1½ cups coconut milk.
5. Boil for 5-6 minutes. Add lemon juice and noodles. Mix well.
6. Serve garnished with fried garlic, spring onions, chillies and coriander leaves.

Note : If serving as a soup, after step 4, boil for 5-6 minutes. Mix in lemon juice. Divide noodles into individual bowls and ladle in the hot soup. Top each bowl with garnishing and serve hot.

Pineapple Fried Rice

Serves 5-6

*This dish is very festive to look at. Served in the pineapple shell, it is sure to be a hit.
Use a ripe pineapple so that the flesh can be scooped out easily.*

1 cup long grain rice - boiled (will give about 3 cups when boiled) & spread out in
a big tray to cool
1 ripe pineapple
200 gms sausages - fried & cut into small pieces
100 gms prawns (small)
2-3 tbsp butter
1 tsp red chilli paste or red chilli powder
1 onion - chopped
3-4 green chillies - chopped, ½ tsp garlic paste
¼ cup boiled peas
2-3 tbsp raisins, 10-12 roasted cashewnuts
½ cup coconut cream (optional)
2 spring onions - chopped along with green part

2 tbsp fish sauce, 1 tbsp soya sauce
1 tsp salt (adjust to taste), 1 tsp pepper
10-15 mint or basil leaves for garnishing

1. Boil rice with a little salt. Drain and spread out to cool.
2. Cut pineapple in half lengthwise. Keep the leaves on and scoop out flesh so that you get two shells with a thin border of flesh attached. Chop half the flesh into small pieces. (store the other half for future use).
3. Fry sausages, cut into small pieces.
4. Heat butter. Add red chilli paste or powder. Fry for a few seconds.
5. Add garlic, onions, prawns and peas. Cook for 2-3 minutes till prawns are done.
6. To step 5 add all ingredients — spring onions, chillies, sausages, raisins, tomato, rice, cashewnuts and also the chopped pineapple pulp.
7. Mix well and cook till rice is well heated.
8. Spoon into pineapple shells. Garnish with mint/basil leaves and serve. Alternately, after mixing rice and other things well (step 7), do not heat rice. Spoon into pineapple shells, cover with aluminum foil and bake.

Crispy Fried Noodles

Serves 4-5

50 gms noodles - either rice noodles or egg noodles can be used. If using rice noodles fry directly but if using egg noodles first boil them & then fry them till crisp.

2 tbsp oil

1 tbsp chopped garlic

1 tbsp chopped shallots/onion

½ tsp red chilli paste

2 tbsp red curry paste (page 18)

100 gm boneless chicken, cut into small pieces or prawns

1 tbsp fish sauce

100 gms mixed vegetables (cauliflower or broccoli, baby corn, capsicum, carrot etc.) - cut into small pieces

3-4 lemon leaves

1 cup coconut milk

1 tbsp vinegar
¾ tsp salt
1 tsp sugar
oil for frying

1. Fry noodles in hot oil, a little at a time, till crisp. Keep in an air tight container. (This can be done a few hours in advance also).
2. Heat oil. Add garlic. Fry for 1-2 minutes.
3. Add onion. Fry till transparent.
4. Add red curry and chilli paste. Fry for 2-3 minutes.
5. Add chicken. Fry for 1-2 minutes. Cover and cook on low heat for 5-6 minutes or till nearly tender.
6. Add mixed vegetables, all the seasonings and coconut milk.
7. Boil on low heat. Cover and simmer till chicken and vegetables are just tender. Do not over cook.
8. Add 3/4 of the fried noodles and mix well.
9. Serve hot garnished with the remaining fried noodles and chopped coriander leaves.

¥ ¥ ¥ ¥

Main Course Dishes

¥ ¥ ¥ ¥

Stir Fried Chicken with Cashewnuts

Serves 4   *Picture on back cover*

200 gms chicken, boneless - cut into small strips
6-8 mushrooms - each cut into 2 pieces
½ tsp salt & ½ tsp crushed peppercorns (adjust to taste)
1 spring onion - cut bulb into 4 pieces and green into 1" long pieces
2 tbsp oil, 1 tbsp chopped garlic, 1" piece ginger - chopped
½ tsp sugar, 1 tbsp fish sauce, ½ -1 tbsp soya sauce
½ green and ½ red capsicum - cut into 1" squares
½ cup freshly roasted or fried cashewnuts, 4 fresh red chillies - slit lengthwise

1. Heat oil in a pan/kadhai. Fry garlic and white part of onion till onion turns light brown. Add ginger. Stir.
2. Add chicken and mushrooms. Add salt and freshly ground pepper. Fry for 4-5 minutes.
3. Reduce heat. Add sugar, fish sauce, soya sauce, green and red capsicums, cashewnuts and red chillies. Saute for 1-2 minutes. Serve hot.

Prawns in Red Curry

Picture on facing page   *Serves 4*

250 gms prawns - use 2"-3" big prawns shelled. However, if these are not
available you can use small ones.
2 tbsp oil, ¾ cup red curry paste (page 18)
2 cups coconut milk, 1 tbsp fish sauce
½ tsp salt, (optional), 1 tsp sugar or gur or 1 tsp soya sauce
4-5 cherry tomatoes or 1 small tomato - cut into 4 pieces
1 tsp lemon juice, 3-4 lemon leaves, ¼ cup basil leaves

1. Heat oil. Add curry paste. Fry for 2 minutes till aromatic and leaves oil.
   Add ¾ cup coconut milk. Boil, stirring constantly.
2. Add fish sauce, salt and sugar. Add the rest of the coconut milk. Boil for
   3-4 minutes. Add prawns and tomatoes. Cook for 3-4 minutes till
   prawns are cooked and curry becomes sligthly thick. Add lemon juice,
   lemon leaves and basil leaves. Boil for 1 minute. Remove from fire.
3. Garnish with chopped chillies and serve hot with steamed rice.

Masaman Curry

Serves 6

This curry can be made with chicken or mutton. For a vegetarian version, use paneer or bean curd. It has a rich, sweet & spicy flavour. Serve with boiled rice.

700-800 gms chicken - cut into small pieces (can be boneless or with bones), 3-4 tbsp oil

2½ cups coconut milk, 1 cup coconut cream

6-8 tbsp heaped masaman curry paste (page 21)

3 tbsp fish sauce

1-2 tsp sugar/gur (adjust to taste)

5 tbsp tamarind juice

6 pods black cardamom (moti illaichi), 2" cinnamon stick

2 medium potatoes - cut into bite size even pieces

1 large onion - cut into wedges & leaves separated

1½ tsp salt, or to taste

½ tsp haldi powder (optional) - gives a better colour if used

50 gms (½ cup) roasted peanuts

1. Heat oil. Add masaman curry paste and ½ tsp haldi. Fry for 2-3 minutes till aromatic and leaves oil.
2. Add chicken. Fry for 3-4 minutes. Add potatoes. Fry for 2-3 minutes.
3. Add coconut cream. Mix well. Cover and simmer till nearly tender.
4. Add coconut milk.
5. Add all other ingredients except roasted peanuts and cook covered on low heat for 6-8 minutes or till chicken and potatoes are fully cooked.
6. Add roasted peanuts. Cook for another 3-4 minutes and serve hot with rice.

Chicken in Red Curry with Mushrooms

Picture on cover   Serves 4-5

400 gm diced boneless chicken (chicken with bones can also be used)
4 tbsp oil
7 tbsp red curry paste (page 18)
2 cups coconut milk
100 gms mushrooms - sliced into thick pieces
1-2 tbsp fish sauce
1½ tsp salt, or to taste
1½ tsp sugar/gur
4-5 lemon leaves
2 stalks lemon grass - tie into a knot (optional)
2-3 fresh green or red chillies - sliced lengthwise
15-20 basil leaves - chopped

1. Heat oil in a wok /pan. Add the prepared red curry paste and stir fry for 3-4 minutes till it gets aromatic and leaves oil.
2. Add chicken, lemon leaves and lemon grass. Fry for 2-3 minutes.
3. Stir in half the coconut milk. Boil. Cover, lower heat and cook till chicken is tender.
4. Add mushrooms. Cook for 3-4 minutes.
5. Add remaining coconut milk and all seasonings. Keep some basil leaves aside for garnishing.
6. Boil, simmer for a 3-4 minutes. Remove lemon grass and lemon leaves.
7. Check salt and adjust to taste.
8. Serve hot garnished with basil leaves.

Note : Although lemon grass is optional, it imparts a very aromatic touch to the dish. You may use only mushrooms if you wish.

Barbecued Chicken

Serves 5-6

Barbecued chicken is served almost everywhere in Thailand, from portable roadside stalls to sports stadiums to beaches. For an authentic touch, serve with rice on a banana leaf.

1 chicken - cut into 8 pieces
2 lemons - cut into wedges
2 green chillies - sliced lengthwise for garnishing
2 tbsp oil

MARINADE

2 stalks lemon grass - cut into pieces
1" piece ginger - chopped, 8-10 large flakes garlic
4 spring onions alongwith green part
½ cup coriander leaves
½ cup coconut milk, 2 tbsp fish sauce
1 tbsp black peppercorns, 1 tsp salt

1. To make the marinade, put all the ingredients given under marinade in the mixer/grinder and grind to a smooth paste.
2. Give deep cuts on the washed chicken pieces.
3. Mix the chicken well with the marinade and let it marinate for 5-6 hours or preferably overnight in the fridge.
4. Grill chicken till well done and crisp. Keep turning the pieces over and brush with the marinade and oil occasionally, or keep on a baking tray and bake at 200°C/400°F for about 25-30 minutes or till chicken is well cooked and crisp.
5. Garnish with lemon wedges, sliced chillies and serve.

¥ ¥ ¥ ¥ ¥
¥
¥
¥
¥

Green Chicken Curry with Aubergine

Picture on page 2　　　　　　　*Serves 5-6*

Although the combination is a little odd but it tastes delicious.

150 gms aubergine (preferably) use the small green variety. However the ordinary purple one can also be used.

3 tbsp oil

5-6 heaped tbsp green curry paste (page 20)

400 gms chicken - boneless or with bones - cut into bite size pieces

2½ cups coconut milk

2 tbsp fish sauce

2-3 lemon leaves

1 tsp sugar/gur

1 tsp salt

10-12 basil leaves chopped

2-3 green/red chillies - slit long for garnishing

1. Heat oil in a pan. Add green curry paste. Fry for 2-3 minutes.
2. Add chicken and again fry for 2-3 minutes.
3. Add 1 cup coconut milk, lower heat and simmer for 4-5 minutes or till chicken is nearly done.
4. Add salt, sugar, basil, fish sauce, lemon leaves, brinjal and the rest of the coconut milk.
5. Boil. Cover and cook on low heat till brinjal and chicken are well cooked.
6. Garnish with sliced green chillies (long thin slices), basil leaves and serve hot with boiled/steamed rice.

Stir fried Chicken with Basil & Chillies

Picture on facing page   *Serves 5-6*

This quick & easy dish is an excellent introduction to Thai cuisine. Deep frying basil leaves adds a different dimension to the dish.

500 gm chicken, boneless or with bones - cut into bite size pieces
2-3 tbsp oil
6-8 flakes garlic - chopped
4 dried, red chillies - whole and 6-8 fresh green chillies - chopped
3-4 tbsp red or 2-3 tbsp green curry paste (page 18, 20)
2 tbsp fish sauce
2 tsp soya sauce (adjust to taste)
1 tsp sugar/gur
10-12 basil leaves

GARNISHING
20 basil leaves - deep fried (optional)

1. Heat oil in a wok or frying pan.
2. Add garlic and chillies (red whole and chopped green chillies). Fry for 1-2 minutes till garlic is golden brown.
3. Add curry paste and fry well. Add chicken. Stir fry till it changes colour. Cover, lower heat and cook till tender.
4. Add all seasonings but do not add fried basil leaves.
5. Stir fry for another 3-4 minutes. Remove from fire.
6. For garnishing, fry basil leaves. Before frying basil leaves make sure they are absolutely dry. Deep fry in hot oil for about 30-40 seconds, lift out of oil and drain on kitchen paper.
7. Garnish the chicken with red chillies and fried basil leaves.

Note : No salt has been added as the salt in fish sauce and soya sauce is enough. However taste it and add as required.

Thai Fish Curry

Serves 3-4   *Picture on page 19*

300 gms fish - cleaned & washed and cut into small (3/4") pieces
3-4 tbsp red curry paste or 2-3 tbsp green curry paste (page18, 20)
2 tbsp oil, 2 cups coconut milk
1 tbsp fish sauce
3-4 lemon leaves
½ tsp salt, 1 tsp sugar/gur (optional)
¼ - ½ cup basil leaves - shredded, 3-4 chillies (green or red) - sliced

1. Heat oil. Add curry paste. Fry for 2 minutes on low heat.
2. Add ½ cup coconut milk. Cook till nearly dry and fragrant.
3. Add fish sauce, lemon leaves, salt and sugar. Add the rest of the coconut milk. Give it one boil.
4. Add fish and basil. Cover and cook for 5-6 minutes, till fish is well done.
5. Garnish with sliced chillies and serve hot with steamed/boiled rice.

Note : Instead of fish, prawns, crabs, paneer and mixed vegetables can be used.

Stir fired Prawns with Vegetables

Serves 3-4

10-12 dried, whole red chillies
200 gm small prawns or 3 - 4" long prawns - shelled and with tail intact
10 babycorns
10 mushrooms (fresh or dried)
2 tbsp oil
1 tbsp chopped garlic
3 tbsp fish sauce, 1 tsp soya sauce
¼ tsp salt, 6-8 peppercorns - crushed
¼ tsp red chilli paste/powder

1. Slice mushrooms into big pieces, cutting each into 2 or 3 pieces.
2. Cut babycorns longitudinally into two pieces and then horizontally into two pieces.
3. Heat oil in a wok/frying pan. Add garlic. Fry for 1 minute.
4. Add salt, red chilli paste/powder. Fry for 1 minute.
5. Add prawns and babycorns. Fry for 2-3 minutes.
6. When nearly cooked (done), add mushrooms, soya sauce and fish sauce. Cook for 2-3 minutes.
7. When mushrooms, baby corn and prawns are done, increase heat, dry and serve garnished with green chillies and crushed peppercorns.

Note : Instead of prawns, use may 200 gm boneless chicken, cut into small pieces or 250 gm chicken with bones, cut into bite size pieces.

If you want a slight gravy, do not dry. After step 6, thicken gravy with 1 tsp cornflour dissolved in 2 tbsp water. Boil and serve.

Garlic Fish

Serves 2-3

Instead of Fish, Prawns, Chicken, Paneer or Mushrooms can be used.

250 gms fish - cut into 1" pieces
2 tbsp chopped garlic
1 tbsp chopped ginger
2 tbsp fish sauce
1 tsp pepper
1½ tsp red chilli paste or powder
1¼ tsp salt
2 tbsp oil
1 tbsp chopped coriander
½ cup (2-3) chopped spring onions
1 tsp garlic paste
1 tsp ginger paste
1 tbsp vinegar or lemon juice

1. Mix together lemon juice, garlic and ginger paste. Marinate fish in it for 1-2 hours.
2. Heat oil in a pan/wok. Add chopped ginger and garlic. Fry for 1-2 minutes.
3. Add red chilli powder.
4. Add spring onions, salt, fish sauce and fish. Cook for 2 minutes.
5. Cover, lower heat and cook for another 2-3 minutes.
6. Increase heat (check if tender), dry. Serve hot, garnished with chopped coriander.

Chicken in Sweet Peanut Sauce

Serves 4-5

*This curry is a little on the sweet side, delicious with a lovely peanut & coconut flavour.
Serve with boiled/steamed rice.*

300 gms chicken - cut into small pieces (can be boneless or with bones)
2 cups coconut milk
5 tbsp red curry paste (page 18)
½ cup roasted & ground peanuts
1 tsp salt
1 tsp red chilli paste
6 lemon leaves
1 tsp sugar
2 tbsp lemon juice/vinegar
2½ tbsp fish sauce
1-2 green/red chillies, thinly sliced - for garnishing

1. Heat ½ cup coconut milk. Boil.
2. Add red chilli paste, red curry paste. Boil till nearly dry.
3. Add chicken. Fry 3-4 minutes.
4. Add all other ingredients except sliced chillies. Add coconut milk.
5. Boil covered. Lower heat and simmer for 8-10 minutes or till chicken is tender.
6. Serve hot garnished with sliced chillies.

Stir Fried Sweet & Sour
Chicken/Fish/Pork/Prawns

Serves 5-6

Sweet & sour is traditionally a Chinese creation, but Thais also do it very well. This flavourful version makes an excellent one dish meal when served over steamed rice.

200 gm chicken - cut into small pieces, can be with or without bones; or pork
sliced thinly or prawns or fish of 1" pieces
3 tbsp oil
5-6 large flakes garlic - chopped, 1 medium onion - sliced
2 tbsp vinegar
2 tbsp fish sauce
1 medium tomato - cut into 1 - 1 ½" long pieces
1 medium capsicum - cut into 1 - 1 ½" long pieces
1 medium cucumber - cut into 1 - 1 ½" long pieces

Tapioca Pudding : Recipe on page 97 ➤

2 tsp cornflour
4 tbsp tomato sauce
½ tsp salt
1 tbsp sugar - adjust to taste
½ - 1 tsp pepper - adjust to taste
½ cup tinned pineapple - cut into chunks

GARNISHING
2 spring onions - sliced diagonally into 1½" length
some fresh coriander leaves

1. Heat 3 tbsp oil. Add garlic. Fry till brown.
2. Add chicken. Stri fry for 3-4 minutes.
3. Add onion. Cover and cook on low heat till chicken/pork is tender. If using prawns or fish this is not required as they cook very fast and step 2 plus latter cooking is enough for them.
4. Add vegetables. Fry for 3-4 minutes or till they are crunchy tender.
5. Add all seasonings. Mix well.
6. Dissolve cornflour in water. Add. Give 1-2 boils. Serve garnished with spring onions and coriander with steamed/boiled rice.

Thai Style Stuffed Baked Chicken

Serves 4

A fancy dish of whole chicken surrounded with rice which makes a complete meal by itself. This decorative dish will most certainly be the centre of attraction.

1 whole chicken (1 kg)

MARINADE
4 tsp garlic paste
4 tsp ginger paste
2 tsp salt
6-8 tbsp lemon juice
3 tbsp soya sauce
2" piece cinnamon (dalchini)
3 star anise
2 tsp pepper
6-7 tbsp red curry paste (page 18)
1 tsp ground nutmeg (optional)
2 tbsp chopped coriander

STUFFING

3 cups boiled rice (cooked) without salt
6 tbsp butter
½ cup chopped onion
6 tbsp red curry paste (page 18)
2 cups chopped mixed vegetables (beans, peas, carrots, cauliflower, broccoli, etc.)
½ cup coconut milk
2 tbsp chopped coriander
1½ tsp salt, or to taste

1. Keep chicken whole, remove skin. Wash well and give deep incissions on the meaty parts i.e., thighs, legs, breasts etc.
2. Mix all the ingredients of the marinade. Rub marinade inside and outside the chicken very well. Leave the chicken to marinate for 3-4 hours or cover and keep in fridge overnight so that the chicken gets well marinated.
3. To prepare the stuffing, heat butter. Add onion. Fry for 2-3 minutes.
4. Add curry paste. Fry for 1-2 minutes.

5. Add vegetables and stir fry for 2-3 minutes.
6. Add coconut milk and salt. Cover and cook till vegetables turn tender.
7. Add rice and coriander. Mix well.
8. Stuff some of the prepared rice in the chicken.
9. Tie legs of chicken with a strip of aluminum foil.
10. Place chicken on a baking tray. Pour all extra marinade on top.
11. Bake in a preheated oven at 190°C for 40-45 minutes or till the chicken is tender.
12. Take out and place on the serving dish (oven proof) surrounded with the rest of the rice and bake again for 10-15 minutes or till the rice is heated thorough.
13. Garnish with boiled egg slices, tomato wedges, lemon wedges and some chopped basil. Serve hot. Cut/slice at the table.

Note : Instead of stuffing rice and also surrounding chicken with rice, you can bake chicken empty and only surround it with rice. Or stuff chicken with stuffing of your choice, for example mashed seasoned potatoes or cooked mince or mixed vegetables and nuts etc.

Batter fried Prawns in Lemon Sauce

Picture on page 1   *Serves 4*

(Kung Sammrot)

8 large prawns with tails intact (chicken or fish can also be used)
8-10 peppercorns - crushed coarsely

BATTER

2 tbsp maida (plain flour), 1 tbsp cornflour, a pinch of baking powder
1 egg, ½ tsp ginger paste, ½ tsp garlic paste
½ tsp salt, ½ tsp pepper, ¼ tsp red chilli powder

SAUCE

6 tbsp honey, 7-8 tbsp (4 lemons) fresh lemon juice, 1/3 cup water
1 tsp grated ginger, 2 tsp crushed garlic
1½ tsp salt, 3-4 lemon leaves, 2 tsp cornflour
a few drops (1-2 drops) of lemon yellow food colouring
1 spring onion - sliced diagonally alongwith the green part
some fresh chopped coriander leaves

1. Mix all ingredients given under batter. Add 3-4 tbsp water to get a thin batter of coating consistency. Keep aside.
2. Heat oil in a frying pan. Dip prawns, holding the tails, in batter. Do not let the batter coat the tail portion. Drop the prawns in hot oil. Fry on medium heat till golden brown. Remove from oil and keep aside.
3. To prepare the sauce, mix all ingredients except the last two — spring onions and coriander.
4. Boil the sauce. Simmer for about 5 minutes till the sauce turns slightly thick and starts to coat the spoon. Remove from fire. Add 1-2 tbsp sugar if too sour. Mix. Add spring onions and coriander leaves. Keep sauce aside.
5. Arrange fried prawns in a serving dish.
6. Heat sauce and pour on top of the prawns. Serve hot sprinkled with crushed peppercorns.

Assorted Vegetables in Red Curry

Picture on inside back cover   Serves 4-6

VEGETABLES
6-8 baby corns - slit lengthwise
2 small brinjals - peeled and diced int ½" pieces (small)
1 small broccoli - cut into small florets
5-6 mushrooms - sliced
¼ cup chopped bamboo shoots (optional)

OTHER INGREDIENTS
3/4 cup red curry paste - page 18
3 cups coconut milk mixed with 1 tbsp cornflour
½ tsp soya sauce
15 basil leaves - chopped or coriander leaves
1 tbsp oil
salt to taste, ½ tsp brown sugar

1. Heat oil in a large pan, add the red curry paste and fry for 2-3 minutes on low heat.
2. Add 2 tbsp of coconut milk. Add vegetables and cook for 2-3 minutes.
3. Add the rest of the coconut milk, soya sauce and chopped basil leaves.
4. Cover and simmer on low heat for 5-7 minutes till the vegetables are tender.
5. Add salt and sugar to taste. Boil for 1 to 2 minutes. Serve hot with steamed rice or noodles.

¥ ¥ ¥ ¥

Desserts

The Thais end their meal always with delicately carved fresh fruits. There is a dessert also with it for formal occasions.

¥ ¥ ¥ ¥

Tapioca Pudding

Serves 3-4   *Picture on page 87*

This pudding made from Tapioca (saboodana) & coconut milk is a very quick & a light dessert. Adjust sweetness to your liking. It is served with some crushed ice added to it, accompanied with chilled fresh fruits.

½ cup tapioca (saboodana), 1 cup coconut milk
1 cup water, 5 tbsp sugar or jaggery (gur), a pinch of salt
finely shredded lemon rind of ½ lemon (optional) used for garnishing

1. Soak saboodana in warm water for 1-2 hours, till they swell up. Drain.
2. Put water to boil in a saucepan. Add sugar/gur and salt.
3. When sugar has dissolved, add saboodana and coconut milk.
4. Simmer for 5-7 minutes. Transfer to a serving bowl. Keep in the fridge.
5. To serve, add crushed ice in the bowl of dessert which thins it a little. Garnish with lemon rind.
6. Serve delicately carved and chilled fruits with it.

Fried Bananas/Apples

Serves 4-5

*These delicious treats are a favourite with everyone. They are sold as snacks &
served as dessert all over Thailand. Instead of Bananas, Apples can be used and are
just as delicious.*

4 ripe bananas
1 egg
½ cup flour (maida)
1 tsp dalchini powder, 1 tsp nutmeg (jaiphal) powder
a pinch of soda-bi-carb
2 tsp butter or oil
2 tsp sesame seeds (til)
3 tbsp powdered sugar
juice of 1 lemon (large)
3 tsp honey (optional)
½ - ¾ cup milk (approx.)
1 tbsp shredded/grated coconut fresh (optional)

1. Peel and cut bananas into 2 pieces longitudinally and then crosswise to get 4 pieces from each banana.
2. Sprinkle 1 tbsp sugar, ½ tsp nutmeg, ½ tsp dalchini and half the lemon juice on them.
3. Make a batter with flour, oil/butter, egg, milk, honey, sesame seeds, coconut, and soda-bicarb. The batter should not be very thin.
4. Mix well till smooth.
5. Heat oil. Dip banana slices in the batter and fry till golden brown.
6. Place on a serving dish and sprinkle rest of the sugar, nutmeg and dalchini powder and lemon juice on them. Serve warm with coconut ice-cream or by themselves.

Note : Fry 2-3 pieces at a time, otherwise they will stick together.

Coconut Custard

Serves 2-3

This traditional dish can be either baked or steamed. It is generally served with fresh mango or any other fruit.

2 eggs
1 tbsp butter for greasing
½ tbsp flour (maida)
½ tsp vanilla essence or rose essence
¼ cup fresh grated coconut (optional)
50 gms/5 tbsp brown sugar
½ cup coconut milk
some mint leaves and icing sugar for garnishing
carved fresh fruit to be served alongwith the custard

¥ ¥ ¥ ¥ ¥

¥

¥ 1. Grease 3 individual bowls or 1 cake tin with butter and keep aside.
¥   Preheated oven to 260°C (a hot oven).
¥ 2. Beat eggs and sugar with an egg beater very well till it becomes thick like
     a custard.
  3. Add vanilla essence, coconut milk.
  4. Beat well.
  5. Mix in grated coconut (fresh).
  6. Mix well. Pour into individual greased 3 bowls or 1 greased cake tin.
  7. Place in a deep tray. Carefully fill tray with hot water to reach halfway
     up the outside of the cups or tin.
  8. Bake in a preheated oven at 260°C for 30-35 minutes or till it is brown
     on the top. A knife when inserted should come out clean.
  9. Remove from oven. Cool. Turn out or if individual cups have been used,
     serve as it is.
 10. Serve chilled, decorated with some icing sugar (sieve it on top) and a
     sprig of mint.
 11. Serve fresh fruit, carved along with the custard.

Note : Preferably use fresh coconut milk. The milk should not very thin.

Coconut & Date Ice Cream

Serves 6

2 cups thick coconut milk, 15 dates - stoned and chopped
1 tbsp cornflour, 3½ tbsp sugar, 200 gms fresh cream

1. Churn dates with a little coconut milk.
2. Dissolve cornflour in a little coconut milk and keep aside.
3. Mix the rest of the coconut milk & sugar in a pan. Add the date mixture. Boil. Add cornflour paste and give one boil. Keep on low flame. Simmer for 2-3 minutes on low flame. Remove from fire and keep aside to cool.
4. Set ice cream in a covered aluminium container in the freezer for 6-7 hours or overnight.
5. Beat cream over ice till light and fluffy.
6. Beat set ice-cream well.
7. Mix with cream and reset for 6-7 hours or overnight.

Note : You may add some freshly grated coconut at the time of mixing cream.

Nita Mehta's BEST SELLERS (Non-Vegetarian)

MICROWAVE Non-Veg.

FAVOURITE Non-Veg.

The Best of **MUTTON**

ITALIAN Non-Veg.

CHINESE Non-Veg.

MORE CHICKEN

SNACKS Non-Veg.

OVEN Non-Veg.

ikka Seekh & Kebab

Mughlai Cooking

The Best of **CHICKEN** Recipes

Low Calorie Recipes Non-Veg.

NEW SERIES BY *Nita Mehta*

Step by Step Photos

Learn to Cook SERIES

All Colour & Hardcover

LEARN TO COOK — Step by Step
CHICKEN
Nita Mehta

LEARN TO COOK — Step by Step
CHINESE
Nita Mehta

LEARN TO COOK — Step by Step
PIZZA & PASTA
Nita Mehta
Vegetarian

LEARN TO COOK — Step by Step
CHOCOLATE
Nita Mehta

LEARN — Step by Step
Food Styling, Garnishing & Table Laying
Nita Mehta